72 POSITIVE AND INSPIRATIONAL QUOTES TO PUT YOUR DAY IN PERSPECTIVE, WITH COMMENTARY!

Leadership * Success * Mindset
Unleashing Your Inner Potential

[Vol 1]

Emmanuel Amoako

Table of Contents

Prologue

L ife is such a beauty, an arena full of a variety of experiences to enjoy, expectations to be met, challenges to overcome and adventures to undertake. But you have realized something is missing. Imagine you have a need that turned out to be the greatest need of all. What if that need when satisfied, would grow into the most deeply rewarding aspect of your life. You do have such a need. How long have you been feeling that inner drive to seek a higher purpose and meaning in your life? It is time to take a leap.

The Devine power, Infinite intelligence or the power that is greater than us in the universe has a way to reward and transform those who stay true to their call and persist to the end. That change, when happened, will propel you towards becoming the-best-version-of-yourself. You do not have to settle for a mediocre life that will diminish your potential and make you invisible to the world. A little dose of daily inspiration is all you need to trigger you into action. This book will help you do just that.

Compiled from the works of some of the most distinguished leaders. Writers, educators, presidents, authors, musicians, philosophers and academics from around the world and throughout history, this book will empower you with wisdom, knowledge, and understanding you need to see the world from a whole new perspective. You will garner the confidence and persistence you need every day to embrace anything life may throw at you. You will acquire insight into the areas of love, leadership, mindset, relationship, entrepreneurship and more. Best of all, the inspiration from these extraordinary men and women and the plan that comes with it that will help you to live a life full of love, hope and promise. You will discover how to enjoy life to the fullest and be the best of who you are meant to be.

Purpose and how to use this book

This writing is to help enlighten your mind to understand the citations and sayings from some of the leading men and women of today and the past. Discover the meaning, secrets, and foresight behind the excerpts of these savvy individuals to unleash the hidden talent and potential in you and be inspired to live your life to the fullest.

For the best results, start your day on a positive note by reading a quote or two, meditate on them as you go through the day. Write down your thoughts and inspiration in the space provided at the back page or in your journal for reference. You can also move straight to the chapters that you think are more appropriate to your area of function or circumstance for a maximum benefit. This will encourage you to stay focus and inspire you to a greater height.

These quotes and many others have helped turn my life around in many ways I never thought was possible. What you are about to read is part of my six years of collection that helped change me to who I am today, more disciplined, well organized, full of confidence, goal-oriented, and purpose-driven. Not to say everything is perfect, but compared to where I was, I have made a lot of progress. I am privileged to share with you the intelligence, insight and perception of these remarkable peoples who have made such an impact in our lives and continue to make. Happy reading.

Quotes and Commentaries

1. True power arises in knowing what you want, knowing what you don't want, expressing it clearly and lovingly without the attachment to the outcome. ~Leonardo Jacobson (Spiritual teacher and author)

Knowing what you want is the first step towards achievement. It's a vast world and often, we do not know what to choose because we have so many options. There are so many ways to make money. There are so many people you can hang out with. There are so many career paths that you could choose. We often exhaust ourselves by not being precise about what we want. Start with your gut and be clear about your goals, vision and purpose, your deepest calling. Start there and you will see that you are no longer cluttered, confused or all over the place.

2. You are who you choose to be – Ted Hughes (The Iron man)

If you take away everything that limits you, all your challenges, fears, issues, who would you be? Now ask yourself, why are you allowing these to stop you? No one's life is free of inhibitions. We all have life challenges that seem to hold us back. Are you someone who is always focused on the problems and get discouraged instead of finding solutions? Do you only see one side of the equation? Do you really believe that the person you desire to be is out of reach?

Listen, life is like a story. There are many ways a chapter could conclude. But what makes the climax is what matters. A house is built one brick at a time. What decisions are you making each day to move you closer to your dreams? The person you are meant to be is hidden inside of you, just dig deeper.

3. Don't be satisfied with what you know, be a lifelong student. ~Indra Noryi (Former CEO of PepsiCo)

If you are unwilling to learn or unlearn, you will not go further than where you are. The mind is a magnificent tool. It has taken mankind to all sorts of heights. Did you ever think you will see the day when you can do virtually anything at the tap of your finger? It is all because humans are made to keep outdoing themselves.

All that happened through learning, testing, analyzing and executing. If you stop doing anything else in this life, never give up learning. You go against your very design if you do.

4. Never spend your money before you have earned it.
~Thomas Jefferson (3rd U. S President)

We buy things we don't need with money we don't have. Look at your life, do you need everything you possess? Do you need that name-brand dress or shoes? Do you need to do your hair every week? Do you need to eat out every day? Material things can be great, but if you are robbing yourself to live a life you cannot afford, it is not worth it. You can live without it, do not buy into advertisements. Take care of your needs. Buy healthy food, pay the necessary bills and cook more. After you cover your needs, save and invest. Be smart with your hard earned money. Tell yourself no more debts, no more living from paycheck to paycheck. And make this a golden rule - if you can live without it, you do not need it.

5. If we lose love and self-respect for each other, this is how we finally die. ~Maya Angelou (American poet, singer and civil right activist)

Respect others and succeed together. Often, it takes a tribe to change the narrative. No man or woman is an island. But if there is no respect for each other, then that tribe will diminish and become barbaric. Every so often one person climbs up to the top and the others get left behind. No community can thrive like that. It takes a village to earn prosperity that spans from generation to generation. Respect each other, look out for each other, stand by each other as we are all in this together.

6. Leadership is action, not a position. ~Donald McGannon (Broadcasting executive)

A leader is just an empty title without execution. You must be what you want to lead. You must get up living that truth. You must show and never just tell because leaders; they cannot help but to do.

7. Leaders must be close enough to relate to others, but far ahead to motivate them. ~John Maxwell (American author and leadership coach)

Leadership is not leading to victory but leading from victory. After the wins, do you let the reigns go? Do you simply relax? No, your team, your tribe still needs you. They need you to show up and take charge of whether it is raining, or the sun is out mighty bright. Leadership never stops just because you just had a win. It is where leadership begins.

8. It's not lack of love but lack of friendship that makes unhappy marriages. ~Friedrich Nietzsche (German philosopher and a cultural critic)

Marriage works when we do it in God's way. If you want to know what love is, read first Corinthians 13 verses 4-8. Love is patient, love is kind, it does not envy one another, it does not boast, it is not proud. It does not dishonor others, it is not self-seeking, it is not easily angered, it keeps no record of wrongs. Love does not delight in evil but rejoices with the truth. It always protects, always trusts, always hopes, always perseveres. Love never fails.'

If we love in the way it was expressed in the Bible, our marriages will not fail. But it takes two. Two people have to commit to love the way God intended.

9. Thinking is the hardest job there is, that's why less people engage in it. ~Henry Ford (American industrialist and a business magnate)

Funny that many choose to think less when we are wired to be critical beings. It is in our design to think, analyze, reflect and address. That is one of our greatest abilities. Do not be afraid of your intelligence. Embrace it and it will take you far.

10. Think big and don't listen to people who tell you tell you it can't be done. Life is too small to think small. ~Tim Ferriss (American author and entrepreneur)

When it comes to your own development, you cannot wait until someone ask us to do it. The onus is on you to develop yourself. While it is great to have support or someone to guide you, it is in your own hands to move from one step to the next. Imagine if trees waited on another tree to tell them to grow, then no tree would be as tall as they are, bear as many fruits as they do or even give shelter to some of the smaller trees who require some shade. Do not wait for others to tell you to grow. You have all that you need inside to do that yourself.

11. Luck is a matter of preparation meeting opportunity. ~Lucius Annaeus Seneca (Roman Philosopher)

No one will truly invest in you but you. As an employee, you might find that you put in as much as is needed to get by. Sometimes, you do exactly what you are paid for, nothing more, nothing less. It is not your company, right? At the end of it all, you will not get as much returns as the business owner. Also, you are disposable.

They can easily replace you. You will have no claim to the creativity you have given or to your intelligent properties.

No, it is all theirs and the rewards are mostly theirs to reap. When you become a business owner, everything shifts. You are putting in 16 or more hours. You are wearing many hats. You are doing all that is necessary to ensure your business thrives. When you hire someone, you realize that they will never put in as much as you. It is not their company, what should they truly invest? If you do not put in all that is needed to take your business from Point A to B, who will? You are your business. You are the CEO of your life. Will you do all that is necessary to make your business thrive or will you watch yourself fall by the wayside?

12. Do not give up, you never know who you are inspiring ~Maxie McCoy (Writer and a speaker)

There was a young woman, an immigrant living in another country. She was alone and homesick. The only job she could get was at a hair salon. This was something she did well at home. Every day before she went to work, she would remember what her mother said, 'You're never fully dressed without a smile'. No matter what life brought her way, she never left her home without putting her smile on.

Memories of her mother helped her pulled through the day. She treated her customers like they were her family, always putting a smile on their faces. One day at work, she felt a sudden pang in her chest. She had no customers at that time, so she rushed from the office to the back of the building. She could not help it. Tears streamed down her face. She missed home, her family, her life she left back in Jamaica. She wanted to give up so badly. But she knew she could not. After crying for about 15 minutes, she wiped her face dry. She put on her smile and went back to her chair. One of her clients entered the salon shortly after.

'Thank you,' she said.

Baffled, the hairdresser asked 'For what? I haven't even done your hair yet.'

'For always encouraging me to embrace life now.'

The hairdresser had no idea what her client was going through, that she had her own battles. She thought this lady had everything going for her. But somehow, she a small island young woman had inspired someone she never dreamed she would just by coming to work every day, smiling and being herself.

People do not always talk about the impact your lives have on them. Often, we inspire others in silence. It could be your next-door neighbor, your employer, your teacher, your partner, your children. Just keep at it because of your mere presence, your mere work, your mere doing sends energy near and far to all those who need it the most.

13. If you are not willing to risk the unusual, you will have to settle for the ordinary. ~Jim Rohn (American entrepreneur and author)

Do not die wandering, life is all risky. We all have obstacles that stand between us and what we want. How many opportunities have we given up to love, grow and become because of our inhibitions? What got you wandering today? Is that man or woman you thought would not like you? Is it that career you believed you were not good enough for? Is it that country you just could not get on the plane for? What is it? And how much does it hurt? Days turn into months and months rush into years. Anything could happen anytime. There is not enough money and highly advanced technology in the world to stop the unexpected from happening.

Many things are beyond our control. You may go to sleep and never again see the sunrise. Do not be anxious, it is a fact of life. You are not alone when it comes to this. The only thing you have control of is yourself, actions and the path you choose to take. Whether or not you submit that application, invite that person to lunch or take that leap of faith. You are making those moves in this game of life.

14. To know what life is worth, you have to risk it once in a while. ~Jean-Paul Sartre (French philosopher and novelist)

Don't ask for security, ask for adventure. We are not saying security is not important. There are some things that you need to be secured. But when you find yourself in an unhappy cycle or get stuck at a level just for the sake of security, you know that is not how you want to live. The adventure opens you up to knowledge you never thought you would have and experiences that mold you. Sometimes it breaks up the concrete that prevents the seed of your purpose to grow. Do not fear being uncomfortable, not having that house, or car. or If you should fear anything, it should be living without purpose, passion or drive. For without those, you will not truly be alive.

15. There are three types of people: those who make things happen, those who watch things happen and

those who don't know what happened. ~Les Brown
(American motivational speaker and author)

Which one are you? Which one have you decided to be? Everything starts and ends with a decision. Are you choosing to go, be a bystander or be clueless? Do you know you have more power over your life than you express? Do you know you can move from clueless to being in charge? You just have to make up your mind to be that type.

16. *Your friends will believe in your potential, but your enemies will make you live up to it. ~Tim Fargo (American author and a keynote speaker)*

The only limit to your potential is you. This is best summed up is a quote by Marianne Williamson who is an American author and activist said, "Our deepest fear is not that we are inadequate. Our deepest fear is that we are powerful beyond measure". It is our light, not our darkness that most frightens us. We ask ourselves, who am I to be brilliant, gorgeous, talented or fabulous? Actually, who are you *not* to be?

You are a child of God. Playing small does not serve the world. There is nothing enlightened about shrinking so that other people will not feel insecure around you. We are all meant to shine, as children do. We were born to manifest the glory of God that is within us. It is not just in some of us, it is in everyone. And as we let our own light shine, we unconsciously give others permission to do the same. As we are liberated from our own fear, our presence automatically liberates others.

Stop playing small. Human beings are made with tremendous potential. It is up to you to act on it.

17. As a man thinketh so he becomes. ~James Allen (British Philosophical writer)

Have you ever thought of something and it happened, good or bad? That is the power of thoughts. Amy Morin, *Psychotherapist, and international bestselling author,* once said

'Your thoughts are a catalyst for self-perpetuating cycles'. What you think directly influences how you feel and how you behave. So, if you think you are a failure, you will feel like a failure. You will act like a failure, which reinforces your belief that you *must be* a failure.

What are you becoming based on your thoughts? What can you become if you thought the opposite of your current thoughts?

18. Until you realize how easy it is for your mind to be manipulated, you remain a puppet of someone else's game. ~Evita Ochel (Author and a visionary speaker)

Jim Rohn once said, "Everyday stand guard at the door of your mind and decide what goes into your mental factory because you've got to live with the results." Do you filter the information you take in daily? Or do you watch, listen, absorb anything or everything? Do you turn away from a page if it will be consumed by your mind and lead to ill thoughts? Do you shut out anything that breaks down your values? Filtering is important. It is like keeping away excess sugar from your body or too much process food. Do not mentally consume what is not good for you.

19. Someone's opinion of you doesn't have to become your reality -Les Brown (American author and a motivational speaker)

"You are not good enough" or "You will never amount to anything" or "You will never make it without education." Everyone has opinions. It is only right for them too. We are all thinking and feeling beings. That is something you cannot prevent and that is fine. Let people think what they think of you. What is important is what you believe of yourself. Filter if necessary, Put up that forte against the attack of other opinions. Let them fire all they want. Remain unbroken, Remain strong. Their opinions are their business. Your life is yours.

20. Pessimist sees difficulty in every opportunity, the optimist sees opportunity in every difficulty -Winston Churchill (Former British Prime Minister)

Pessimism can suck the light out of anything. Even if the sun is shining while it rains, pessimism clouds your vision and all you see is the storm, the damage and you become ruined. While optimist will allow you to see that the rain is necessary for the plants to grow while appreciating the bit of sunshine there is. The thing is life is not without difficulties. No one is exempted from this. How you view it depends on how you want to view it. Are you going to see just the difficulties and miss the blessings?

21. Do one thing every day that scares you. ~Eleanor Roosevelt (Former First Lady of United States)

Take a risk, if you win you will be happy if you lose you will be wise. A nine-month-baby stands up and gets ready to take off. It is his first go ever! He wobbles as he tries to keep steady, his left foot takes off, it is in mid-air. It almost touches the floor and bam, he falls! He tries it over again, this time using his right foot and guesses what happens? He falls again. Do you think that baby will stop? Do you think he will give up after his 15th try? This baby this time uses a chair as support. He ensures he stands up steady then he takes his first half-steady step. Everyone who is watching that baby explodes into laughter and excitement. That is the power of trying. You take a risk, you fall, you learn, you try again, fall down, learn. That wisdom you garnered from the times you fell will eventually lead to success. That is, if you are willing to try again.

22. Before it controls you, control your mind with love and appreciation. ~Dabasish Mridha (American author and philosopher)

If you do not control your mind, your mind will control you and take you on a wild trip. It is easy to go down a rabbit hole when you allow your mind to spiral out of control, but controlling your mind is not as easy as it sounds. It takes time, practice, discipline, and training. You will have to consciously tell yourself that you will choose another way and will not give in to what you feel.

Leadership Inspired

"If your actions inspire others to dream more, learn more, do more and become more, you are a leader."

~ John Quincy Adams (6th U. S President)

****

"Innovation distinguishes between a leader and a follower"

~ Steve Jobs (Investor and co-founder of Apple)

****

"Leadership and leaning are indispensable to each other"

~ John F. Kennedy (35th U. S. President)

****

"The pessimist complains about the wind. The optimist expects it to change. The leader adjusts the sail."

~ John Maxwell (American author and a leadership coach)

****

"A true leader is not a searcher of consensus, but a molder of consensus"

~ Martin Luther King Jr (Civil right Leader and a minister)

****

"A boss has the title. A leader has the people."

~ Simon Sinek (Author and a motivational speaker)

****

"Efficiency is doing the thing right. Effectiveness is doing the right thing"

~ Peter F. Drucker (Austrian-born American consultant)

****

"We cannot lead one farther than we have been
ourselves"

~ John C Maxwell (Author and a leadership coach)

****

"As we look ahead into the next century, leaders will be
those who can empower others"

~ Bill Gates (American business magnate and
philanthropist)

****

"Don't tell people how to do things, tell them what to do
and let them surprise you with their results"

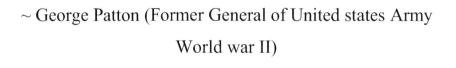

~ George Patton (Former General of United states Army World war II)

Success Inspired

"life is 10% of what happen and 90% of how you react to it."

~ Charles Swindoll (Author and a preacher)

****

"To succeed in life you need two things, ignorance and confidence."

~ Mark Twain (American writer and humorist)

****

"The best revenge is a massive success."

~ Frank Sinatra (American singer and producer)

****

"The path to success is to take massive determined action."

~ Tony Robbins (American author and a life coach)

****

"Success does not come from physical capacity. It comes from an indomitable will."

~ Mahatma Gandhi (Indian lawyer and anti-colonialism)

****

"Every accomplishment starts with a decision to try."

~ John F. Kennedy (35th U. S. President)

****

"If my mind can conceive it, and my heart can believe it, then I can achieve it."

~ Muhammad Ali (American professional boxer and activist)

****

"There is only one way to avoid criticism, do nothing, say nothing, and be nothing."

~Aristotle (Greek philosopher)

****

"Impossible is a word to be found only in the dictionary of fools."
~ Napoleon Bonaparte (French statesman and a military leader)

****

"Every strike brings me closer to the next home run."
~ Babe Ruth (Former American baseball player)

****

"I never dreamed of success, I worked for it."
~ Estee Lauder (Old and wise monk)

****

"There are three things you can do with your life. You can waist it, you can spend it, or invest it. The best use of your life is to invest it in something that will last longer than your time on earth."
~ Rick Warren (American pastor and author)

Quotes and Commentaries

23. In the end, we will only regret the chances we didn't take. ~Lewis Carroll (English writer)

Can you imagine yourself 30 years or older? What do you think will be important then? If your older self could write a letter to you, what would it say? Would that person be happy that you did not start your business? Would that person be content that you did not choose to go to that country? Would it agree with you not choosing a life that you can be in love with? Think about that. You 5 or 10 years from now, what account will it give? Every day you are writing that book of your life. Every day you are filling the pages with the characters, the plot, the scenery, the lessons. Are you writing a chapter that is riddled with regret or fulfillment?

24. It's not only possible to achieve your dreams, it's necessary -Les Brown (Author and a motivational speaker)

Who are you without dreams? Your dreams, goals, and purpose bring meaning to your life. It pumps your desire for life and living. Without having a dream, accomplishing even some of them, life would be tasteless, colorless and overall, empty. You have a right to dream and the courage to chase them. You have a right to life and the power to change it.

25. Keep the main thing the main thing. ~Stephen Covey (American educator and author)

A striker is never the goalie in football. A striker's main aim is to focus on shooting. If you are trying to cover other positions, you are distracting yourself from your main goal. Trying to cover other positions will distract you from your main purpose, which is to shoot and score. Eyes on the goal so that you can shoot to score when the ball gets to you.

26. Change your mindset, change your life. ~Unknown

Many of us hold a fixed mindset. We believe in certain things, whether these prove to be true or not. Our thoughts though intangible finds in its physical form through us. You are what you believe you are. Do this exercise, write down 5 positive and negative things about yourself. After you have finished that, write down actual experiences that depict the things you wrote down.

It is no wonder changing your mindset can be so difficult, after all this is who you are, a reflection of your mentality. How do you tell yourself to undo all you have been and did for years? In fact, you cannot undo what is done. What is in the past is in the past. However, you can choose a different path by first thinking about what you want to change and coming up with a plan to change it.

For example, suppose you love to spend all the money you have and therefore cannot save. How do you change from spending all to saving more? First, mentally decide what you want to save. Then decide how you want to do it. What are the benefits? What material can you read, watch, listen to that will encourage this change thought and behavior? Changing your mindset takes more than thinking. You have to do and do so repeatedly until this change becomes you.

27. In the middle of every difficulty, lies an opportunity. ~Albert Einstein (German-born theoretical physicist)

Keep trying and the universe will give way to you. Meditate on what you want and keep going for it. The universe has a way of opening doors of opportunity to those who persuade it through thoughts and actions. Manifestation does not just happen overnight. It takes time, work and dedication. You cannot be tempted by quick rewards. It does not always work that way, success takes time.

28. Becoming what you want is as simple as trying.
~Steven Redhead (Musician)

Once you stop fighting for what you want, what you do not want will take over. You know what you want in a relationship, so you spent most of your 20s not committing because you have not seen what you are looking for. You keep aiming for the promise you made to yourself, the standards you set for yourself. It is so close yet so far. Whenever you go on a date and realize that person is just not the one, the search gets tiresome and you become weary.

A red flag came up and you made that slide. The person lied. It is just one simple lie, you tell yourself. It will not happen again, then it does. You made that slide too. You have been searching for too long. You begin to believe that what you want does not exist and settled for less than you deserve. Two lies turn into too many and before you know it, you are in a relationship with someone who lies all the time. That was a deal-breaker for you when you started out. Now you are miserable and unhappy but committed to what you do not want because you gave-up on what you want.

29. Greatness is a choice, but most people choose no. ~Anthony Moore (British musical composer)

Oprah Winfrey, Richard Branson, Walt Disney, Albert Einstein – What do these four people have in common? They could have been deterred by the failures in their lives and never been known for whom they are today. If greatness was a destiny, they would have been on a clear path for greatness from the beginning? How many times have they tried, failed and decided to go again? That is where the choice comes in. You can choose to create excellence or otherwise.

30. I have found out that if you love life, life will love you back. ~Arthur Rubinstein (American-Polish classical pianist)

You cannot get out of life alive, so you may as well have a good time. To get out of life means having no life at all. So why not enjoy while it is here? Watch the sunrise, get a massage, walk on the beach, savor the taste of your favorite food, smell the roses, make love to life.

31. To the pessimist the glass is always half empty. To the optimist, the glass is always half full -Jim Rohn (Author and a motivational speaker)

Perspective is everything. You are going to be met with all sorts of challenges. How you view it depends on you. Do a little experiment. Take glass out, pour water into it until it is halved. You decide if it is half-full or half-empty. The answer will depend on your mindset.

32. In the end, you should always do the right thing even if it's hard. ~Nicholas Sparks (American romance novelist and screenwriter)

It is easy to be your best self when everything is going well. No worries, no problems then it is a party up in here! You shine bright like a diamond and everyone loves you. But what happens when things get sour? Do you even recognize yourself?

Let's face it! Some of us buckle under pressure. We behave the opposite of who we are when faced with obstacles. Does that make you less? As humans that give us an opportunity for growth and character building. All we have to do is choose to be consistent.

33. A joy that's shared is a joy made double, Shared sorrow is half a sorrow. ~Swedish proverb

We all have some exciting moments and experiences which bring magical memories. When you accomplish something and you share it with a family, friend or partner, how does that make you feel? Do you feel that energy that lights up among you all? If you had an issue before, that joy supersedes or even provides an avenue to solve it.

34. Works and not words are the proof of love. ~English Proverb

Words are great but they often are not enough without actions. It is also easy to say anything without meaning to what you said. When you express through actions, that is evidence that you are true to your words.

35. When you were born, you cried, and the world rejoice. Live your life in such a manner that when you die the world will cry and you rejoice. ~Indian Proverb

This quote is pretty profound. Leaving this world is an inevitable act. But before you go, how will you live it? Who will you impact? What memories will you make with others and for yourself? At the end of it all, you want to be able to look back and think "I lived life the best I could. I've fulfilled my purpose. I've really loved, laughed, put my all into this earthly experience now I am fine with leaving." It is all about how we spent our days in the world that impacts how we end it.

36. The future belongs to those who believe in the beauty of their dreams. ~Eleanor Roosevelt (Former U. S first lady)

Les Brown once said, "For you to achieve your dream, you got to stay hungry."

When was the last time you were hungry? How did you feel? And how did it motivate you to do what you can to get food? And I am not just talking about hunger for food, but hunger to pursue your purpose and dreams. Do you know you can stop hustling now? Staying hungry gives many of us fuel to keep leveling up and making the greatest version of ourselves and dreams a reality.

37. Tough times don't last, but tough people do. ~Robert Schuller (American pastor and a motivational speaker)

Everything is for a time. No problem lasts forever. The question is can you hold on to see it through? Tupac said, "If you can make it through the night there is a brighter day." It takes a whole lot of strength sometimes to make it through the night, but you will be stronger and better for it. Do not give up, you are a winner.

38. The true character of a man is what he does when no one is watching. ~John Wooden (Former NBA player and a coach)

Who are you behind closed doors? Who are you when you are alone, away from the influence and the desire to put on a mask? Do you like that person or not? If you do not, remember you have the power to change it.

39. Never whine, never complain, never try to justify yourself. ~Robert Greene (American author)

Your attitude determines your altitude! In his book "Learned Optimism", Dr. Seligman found that negative people make less money after doing a long-term study of 1500 people. It is time to check your attitude! It could be the reason why you never go further than where you are right now. If you are grateful, you will see God open up new doors. A strong positive mental attitude will create more miracles than any wonder drug.

40. Value has a value only if its value is valued. ~Brian Taylor (Former CEO of Coca Cola)

It sounds like a tongue-twister but its meaning is straight-forward. If you do not value something, it does not matter how much it is worth, you will not find it valuable. For instance, in this age of social media where attention is a drug and integrity (though crucial) is not valued by many because it is not worthy to those who will do anything for the attention.

41. Life doesn't give you what you want it will give you what you deserve. ~Tarun Sharma

If you plant nothing, will you expect to reap fruits and vegetables? If you do not train for the race, do you expect to win? Ask Usain Bolt, he will tell you the answer to the latter.

42. It's better to prepare for an opportunity that never comes than to have an opportunity and not prepared - Les Brown. (American author and a motivational speaker)

Are you prepared to be successful or are you prepared to fail? Success takes preparation and when that meets opportunity, you have scored. However, if you are unprepared when opportunity knocks at your door, it will walk away. Maybe it will return. Maybe it will not. If you were ready the first time, there would be no maybes.

43. Life is a challenge, meet it! Life is a dream, realize it! Life is a game, play it! Life is love, enjoy it! ~Sathya

Sai Baba (Indian guru and a leader of the religious movement)

There are some unwritten rules to life. These are set by humans. Before you can master these rules, you first have to know what these are. You have to study, review, observe, absorb then practice and practice some more.

44. It doesn't matter how you started but how you end.
~Dr. Eliezer Gonzalez (Good News Unlimited)

The one-time richest man in the world, Bill Gates said, "If you are born poor, it's not your fault, but if you die poor it's your fault"

Our start (the literal start) is not within our control. Some people are born into the worst conditions. Some people are born with disadvantages. That is not within your control, but the race of life should be. Before you end, you decide how you want to end by doing what is necessary for that ending. Your destiny is in your hand, strive for the best you are meant to be.

45. *It doesn't matter how long you live but how well you do it. ~Martin Luther King Jr (Preacher and a civil right activist)*

Who knows how long you will live! If we take each day as it is and make the most of it, we can put a lot of years into 24 hours.

46. *He who is not courageous enough to take risks will never accomplish anything in life -Muhammad Ali. (Professional boxer and activist)*

It takes a lot of guts to do something when you cannot be entirely sure how it will work out. It could go down south very quickly or work out tremendously well for you. How will you know if you do not take a step? Every successful person understands taking the risk is one the main path to accomplishment.

47. The riches that are in the heart can never be stolen. ~Oscar Wilde (Irish poet and playwriter)

You could buy the most expensive thing and employ the tightest security, there is always the slightest possibility of it being stolen. Physical riches can come and go. Sometimes, it does easily. But what is in heart stays with you forever and it is priceless.

48. Act quickly, think slowly ~James Allen (British philosophical writer)

Taking your time to think is a necessary skill you need to have if you want to be successful. It gives you clarity and eliminates the confusion, so when the moment is right to act, you do not hesitate. This will give you a higher chance of success because the opportunity does not wait around forever.

49. Teachers point to the door, but you must enter by yourself -Chinese Proverb.

Teachers are great and some are the best facilitators we know. They provide great advice, guidance and connect the path from data to information. For some, teachers can be like parents, but they are not there to hold your hand or spoon-feed you throughout the journey. They provide you with the tools you need to build your own life with your own hands. Do not miss out on the guidance they provide but at some point, you should be ready to take your destiny into your own hands.

Reading Inspired

"My best friend is a person who will give me a book I
have not read."

~ Abraham Lincoln (16th U. S. President)

****

"Show me a family of readers, and I will show you the
people who move the world."

~ Napoleon Bonaparte (French statesman and a military
leader)

****

"How can any man judge unless his mind has been
opened and enlarged by reading.'

~ John Adams (2nd U. S. President)

****

"Once you learn to read, you will be forever free."

~ Frederick Douglass (American orator and abolitionist)

****

"Not all readers are leaders, but every leader is a reader.'

~ Harry Truman (33rd U. S. President)

****

"A reader lives a thousand lives before he dies. The man who never reads lives only one."

~ George R.R Martin (American novelist)

****

"Reading is essential for those who want to rise above the ordinary."

~ Jim Rohn (Author and a motivational speaker)

****

"You can never get a cup of tea large enough or a book long enough to suit me."

~ C.S Lewis (British writer and a lay theologian)

****

"Think before you speak. Read before you think."

~ Fran Lebowitz (American author and public speaker)

****

"Always read something that will make you look good if you die in the middle of it."

~ P.J. O'Rourke (Journalist and a political satirist)

****

"Make it a rule never to give a child a book you would not read yourself."

~ George Bernard Shaw (Irish playwriter and a critic)

****

Quotes and Commentaries

50. *Experience is the best teacher and the worst experiences teach the best lessons. ~Harry Callahan (American educator and photographer)*

Speaking of teachers, life has a lot. They might be your parents, other family members, friends, and even strangers. The lessons they learned through their own mistakes can be shared with you. All the lessons you could learn, at someone else's expense. You do not have to go through it to know it.

51. *A misty morning doesn't signify a cloudy day. ~Ancient proverb*

We see it often. Something may start out poorly but can turn out to be the best experience. Things are not always the same as they appear. The sun is not shining on a particular morning. It might be cloudy or looks like it is going to rain. You may have canceled your plans or decided to take a different route just in case it rains. Then suddenly, the sun bursts out of nowhere, bright and smiling fully at you. Unexpected, right? That is the beauty of life.

52. Love is the force capable of transforming an enemy into a friend -Martin Luther King Jr. (Minister and a civil right activist)

Love can move mountains. It sweeps hatred away and melts animosity. It breaks barriers. It is not biased or clings to a particular race. Love is just and powerful. If we operate from the heart and continuously do so, we are inspiring and eventually liberating others to do so. Hatred has no way of growing if its roots are not being watered.

53. Even the highest towers begin from the ground - Chinese proverb

Every major success has a humble beginning. When we were children, we were taught about the building. Most of our parents bought us building blocks. We learn to put one on top of the other until it gets tall or we run out of blocks. As babies, we begin as laying in our parents' arm then we get to move a limb or two, then to crawling, walking, running swimming until some of us become Olympians. It would not have happened if we did not start crawling. Whatever your dreams are you have to start somewhere, even if it is small.

54. There are more treasures in books than all the pirate's loot on Treasure Island. ~Walt Destiny (American entrepreneur and animator)

Books are the tools that ignite the heavens of your mind. It does not matter what type of books you like, fiction or non-fiction, short stories, novels, plays, prose, poetry or drama…merely reading a book takes us beyond ourselves. For many, books help a lot. It takes you from low self-esteem to self-confidence, from ignorant to knowledgeable, from barely earning to earning enough.

Some of the most successful people will tell you that they read and often too. One of the first things many people recommend when you are seeking a mindset change, career change, even relationship change is to read extensively. Even if you are reading purely for pleasure, it is the kind of high you cannot describe and want to visit again and again. Commit to reading more as much as you can, in any form you can. There are so many options now to listen to a story that you never have to miss out on. Find one that works for you.

55. We are the sum total of our experiences. ~B. J. Neblett (American author)

It is no secret as they say, "If you hang out with nine broke people, you are likely to be the tenth." Let's admit it, people affect us. People rub off on us especially if we are around them often. Ever found yourself saying a certain phrase, thinking or acting in a way you would not normally do? Did it hit you that is how your close friend or family member acts? We are all connected especially those you align with the most.

Sometimes, you have to assess your inner circle. Who are the people you are hanging around with and how are they affecting your life? Are they adding value to your life and you adding value to theirs? Do you find that you all have similar situations or influence each other to have similar happenings? It is good to look at who you are around and how you all affect and reflect on each other.

56. People take different roads seeking fulfillment and happiness. Just because they are not on your road doesn't mean they've gotten lost. ~Dalai Lama (Spiritual leader of the Tibetan people)

If you want to be who others want you to be, who is going to be you? When it comes to choosing careers, some people are not making their own choices. They might want to be a doctor, lawyer or entrepreneur because their parents, friends or partners want them to be. Are you that person? Deep down, many might not, that is not their career. It is great but not the one you want.

It is not always easy to decipher what you want especially when you are trying to please others. However, choosing something like a partner might turn out to be a lifetime decision. It is something you might have to live with for a long time. Deciding what you want for yourself is crucial to your success and happiness.

57. Knowing yourself is the beginning of all wisdom - Aristotle (Greek philosopher)

Influence can be like a disease. You have people telling you who you should be or who you are. If you allow it to, that can eat away your identity. Yet knowing who you are is not a black or white concept. It takes time and can get complicated.

Lack of self-awareness can be a very painful mistake. Take time to know yourself, vision, dreams, and purpose. Know what you want and why you want it. Others might try to define you but once you know who you are, you are forever free and will not make any impact on you.

58. Attribute my success to this: I never took nor gave excuses. ~Florence Nightingale (English social reformer and statistician)

Success comes before woke only in the dictionary. This is alphabetically true, but in real life, success hardly just comes to you without putting in the work first. It is easy to wish for prosperity but working for it is one of the most crucial steps in its attainment.

59. Not all readers are leaders, but all leaders are readers. ~Harry S. Truman (33rd U. S. President)

Reading opens your mind to independent thinking. It encourages you to question. It encourages you to think beyond what you see. It inspires you to go ahead. The more substantial material you read, the more it encourages your independent thoughts. You will acquire more knowledge, know what you can explore, improve good ideas, create better ideas, turn it all into reality. Never doubt the power of reading.

60. He who forgives ends the quarrel -African proverb

It takes two to argue. If one is not engaging, the other will likely stop. If one does not express anger, the other will likely stop. If the other person moves on, the other will likely do the same. Make a choice to choose the best for you, your joy and peace of mind and the other person will likely do that too.

61. It is with our judgment as it is with our watches, no two go just alike, yet each believes his own. ~Alexander Pope (English poet)

No matter how good or bad you fry a pancake; it is going to have two sides. Everyone has their side of the story. Some people express that side, some do not. Before you start to judge or make a conclusion, do remember there is a side you just have not heard and probably never will if the person chooses not to tell.

62. There is no pillow so soft as a clear conscience - French proverb

You sleep like a bear when you have nothing to hide. That is something we should all aim for – a clear conscience. If you are not clear, it will be like there are swords in your bed.

63. Pay attention to little things, the kite flies because of its tail -Hawaiian proverb

It is the little things that make the big things work. It might be as simple as having warm lemon tea in the morning or snuggling at nights. It could be having post-it with your to-dos or spending a few minutes with your dog. It could be having homecooked meals instead of eating out or taking a few minutes out to examine yourself. It could be reading 15 minutes a day or exercising 15 minutes. Whatever it is, the big things – your goals, relationships and more. Acknowledge and appreciate those little things.

64. Feed your fears and your faith will starve. Feed your faith and your fears will. ~Max Lucado (American pastor and author)

Every time you tell your fears no, you are nurturing your faith. You are letting your fears know that these are not bigger than the positive things you believe in. You are letting them know that they do not matter as much. You are giving them less and less energy, so these begin to shrink as your faith grows. And when your faith grows, so does the goodness of your life.

65. If you believe it, you can achieve it. ~Darius Foroux (Self-helped writer)

If you tell yourself, you want to be a dancer even though you cannot dance well, eventually, you will be a dancer if you keep trying. You will train more, learn new moves, conquer old ones, etc. As you express this belief in yourself, you are automatically lighting this belief in others. They now think you can do it because you said you will.

66. It always seems impossible until it's done. ~Nelson Mandela (Former President of South Africa)

You will never know what you can do until you try. Who is steering this ship, flying this plane? Fear can be very crippling, and doubt can easily fade your dreams away. All you need to do is to take a leap of faith and a new horizon will appear.

67. Believe you can, and you are halfway there - Theodore Roosevelt (26th U. S. President)

It takes confidence, faith, and trust in yourself to start. If you never start, you will never get there. If you do not have a belief in yourself, you will never start. Your belief will then influence your behavior and will likely result in the outcome of that belief.

68. The fastest way to get rich is to get rich slowly. ~Warren Buffet (American business magnate and philanthropist)

They say money that comes quickly goes quickly. For instance; several lottery winners became broke within a couple of years of winning. There is a psychology to it all. Getting rich slowly especially for those who were never rich before gets you accustomed to large sums of money, so you will do better with saving, investing and turning it over. You are teaching yourself money management as you go along. You are also choosing concrete, long-term avenues of growing what you already have. Therefore, you will always have a substantial amount of money and you will know how not to lose it so easily.

69. The glory is not in never falling but in rising every time we fail -Chinese proverb

We all fall and if we stayed fallen, we would never see what comes next. Failure is a part of life. A matter of fact, failure can be like a facilitator. But you will never know if you do not brush yourself off and go again and again. You might fail today but there is always tomorrow. Do not forget that your today is not the next day.

70. In order to succeed, your desire for success must be greater than your fear of failure -Bill Cosby. (American stand-up comedian and actor)

Fear is part of our human nature, but we have the power to overcome it and do incredible things. We only have one life to live to achieve our dreams. Do you want to spend it being crippled by fear? Think about that! Every day we are getting older. Every day the days are getting less. If you do not start now, it may be too late.

You are doing this despite the doubts, despite the nervousness, despite the possible embarrassment and you are doing this now. Your dreams are worth more than your worst feelings. Your dreams are worth the shot. Your goals are more important than the fear you feel. Remember what is important and tell fear, not this time!

71. If people aren't calling you crazy, you aren't thinking big enough. ~ Richard Branson (British business magnate and investor)

Think big, do big and win big. Every day you are presented with an opportunity to do phenomenal things. It does not always turn out that way but that should not dissuade you. If you live your life expecting absolutely no challenges, you will not be able to think big. These are the very challenges that inspire us to think beyond ourselves, present circumstances, mediocre solutions. Obstacles put you in a corner and shout at you – hit me with your best shot! Just aim and go for it.

72. If you work hard on your job, you make a living. If you work hard on yourself, you can make a fortune - Jim Rohn (Author and a motivational speaker)

Do let your fears allow you to choose job security over adventure. Are you aiming to make just a living or more than that? The choice is really yours. And whatever choice you make, be prepared to live with the consequences forever. It is perfectly okay to choose to make a living if that is what you want. Remember, five years from now, you will arrive. The question is, where?

You have to be willing to work on yourself. When you do, you will discover what is hidden inside of you, the real you that you never knew existed. This richness of a renewed perspective, new skills, opportunities, experiences will be yours forever. Strive to be the best you are meant to be and deserve.

Love Inspired

"The strongest love is the love that can demonstrate its fragility"

~Paulo Coelho (Brazilian lyricist and novelist)

****

"A flower can't blossom without sunshine, and a man can't live without love."

~Max Muller (German philologist and orientalist)

****

"There is a place you can touch a woman that will drive her crazy. Her heart." ~Melanie Griffith (American actress)

****

"True love stories never have endings."

~Richard Bach (American writer)

****

"Love is friendship set to music."

~Jackson Pollock (American painter)

****

"Love is that condition in which the happiness of another person is essential to your own."

~Robert Heinlein (American science-fiction writer)

****

"We waste time looking for a perfect lover, instead of creating the perfect love." ~Tom Robbins (American novelist)

****

"Love is the greatest refreshment in life."

~Pablo Picasso (Spanish painter and stage designer)

****

"Unless you love nothing else makes any sense."

~E. E. Cummings (American poet)

****

"There is no remedy for love but to love more."

~Henry Thoreau (American philosopher and essayist)

Write down your thoughts and what motivates and inspires you to take action

Acknowledgments

Thanks to God Almighty for the wisdom and understanding to put this together. Dr. John Tuffour and Rev Pastor Charles Owusu for your guidance, directions and encouragement. Also, to these great men and women whose wisdom, knowledge and understanding have shaped and defined our world today. We are forever grateful for your contribution.

Printed in Great Britain
by Amazon

46693490R00047